access

| Abschlussband |

5

KLASSENARBEITSTRAINER

für Schülerinnen und Schüler
mit Lösungen und Lerntipps

Vokabeltrainer-App

Verfügbar für: iOS, Android und Windows Phone

 Dein Online-Angebot enthält: Audios und Lösungen.
Du findest alles auf scook.de.
Dort gibst du den unten stehenden Zugangscode
in die Box ein.

Dein Zugangscode auf
www.scook.de | avzsh-7r5dw

Cornelsen

Inhalt

Unit 1	Australia – country and continent	4

Klassenarbeit A Reading · Words · Language · Speaking · Mediation	5
Klassenarbeit B Listening · Words · Language · Writing	11

Unit 2	Relationships	18

Klassenarbeit A Listening · Words · Language · Writing	19
Klassenarbeit B Reading · Words · Language · Mediation · Speaking	23

Unit 3	Big dreams – small steps	30

Klassenarbeit A Reading · Words · Language · Mediation · Speaking	31
Klassenarbeit B Listening · Words · Language · Writing · Mediation	37

Unit 4	It's up to you	42

Klassenarbeit A Listening · Words · Language · Writing	43
Klassenarbeit B Reading · Words · Language · Mediation · Speaking	47

More help	54
Generelle Lerntipps	59
Bewertungsraster	60
Notentabelle	61
Tracklist	62

Here we go!
Vor dir liegt der **Klassenarbeitstrainer**, der dich bei der Vorbereitung auf die Klassenarbeit unterstützt.
Du findest zu jeder Unit zwei Klassenarbeiten, mit denen du alle Fertigkeiten (skills) trainieren kannst.

Wenn eine Klassenarbeit angekündigt wird, erstelle dir mithilfe der Pläne zum Selbstausfüllen zu Beginn jeder Unit einen Lernplan.
Die **Lösungen**, die du auf www.scook.de findest, enthalten ein Muster.

| Datum | 22. November |

Was kommt dran?

Unit 2: Listening, Vokabeln, *giving advice*, Mediation, Statistiken interpretieren

Datum	Was ich lernen will	Erledigt?	Was ich noch einmal wiederholen muss/ wichtige Hinweise
11.11.	Lernplan erstellen	✓	
12.11.	Vokabeln Unit 2 wiederholen: 1. Teil	✓	

Alle Lösungen sowie die Hörtexte für die Listeningaufgaben 🎧 und Mustertexte für die meisten Speakingaufgaben 💬 findest du online auf www.scook.de. Dort gibst du den Code von Seite 1 dieses Heftes ein.

Lege dir für die Arbeit mit dem Klassenarbeitstrainer ein Schreibheft an, in dem du Schreibaufgaben und andere Übungen notierst.

Für die mit diesem Symbol **More help** gekennzeichneten Aufgaben findest du zusätzliche Hilfen auf S. 54–58. Wenn du diese Hilfe nutzt, führt dies zu Punktabzug bei der Aufgabe.
Vergleiche deine Lösungen mit den möglichen Lösungen sehr gründlich.
Hole dir bei Unklarheiten Hilfe, sodass du erfolgreich üben und lernen kannst.
Du kannst natürlich auch in den *Skills Files* und *Grammar Files* deines Schülerbuches nachschlagen, wenn du etwas nicht mehr genau weißt.
Deine Punktezahl bei *Writing-*, *Speaking-* und *Mediation-*Aufgaben kannst du mithilfe der Bewertungsraster auf S. 60 in diesem Heft ermitteln.
Der Punkteschlüssel auf S. 61 hilft dir, deinen Lernstand einzuschätzen.

Übrigens: Die Klassenarbeiten in diesem Heft prüfen das Gelernte sehr ausführlich ab. Du benötigst daher für die Bearbeitung länger als eine Schulstunde. Natürlich kannst du die Klassenarbeiten auch in „Portionen" aufteilen oder gezielt Übungen auswählen.

Ich wünsche dir viel Erfolg beim Lernen mit deinem Klassenarbeitstrainer.

Katrin Häntzschel

1 Unit
Australia – country and continent

Mein Lernplan

Datum

Was kommt dran?

Datum	Was ich lernen will	Erledigt?	Was ich noch einmal wiederholen muss/wichtige Hinweise

Unit 1

Klassenarbeit A   Gesamtpunktzahl ☐ /68

1 READING The Stolen Generations – a long way to recognition   /6

After watching the film 'Long Walk Home' you want to find out more about native people in Australia and the Stolen Generations. You find an interesting article about the topic on the internet.

Read the text.

www.interesting-facts-Australia.au

At the end of the 19th century, the Australian government introduced laws to improve the lives of the Aborigines. If you were a native child living between 1905 and 1971 in the dry and rocky outback, you would have been included in these improvement plans. Unfortunately, instead of being a period of development for you and your family, these
5 years became one of the most turbulent periods in Aboriginal history. During this time, the government kidnapped generations of innocent native children and permanently separated them from their parents. They put them into overcrowded boarding schools and forced them to give up their Aboriginal identities. It is not difficult to imagine how homesick and scared these children must have felt, especially when they were forced to
10 learn the English language which was completely foreign to them. We know through first-hand reports that the children were traumatized by these dramatic events in their lives. Not unexpectedly, they lost their families forever when they were taken away. We refer to them as the Stolen Generations.

Although many Australians today discuss their native history openly, there is a lot of
15 tension in the discussion. This rough period of history may shock many people, but some conservative politicians defend government actions by arguing that back then, they were actually necessary for protecting the bush natives. In 1997, when the government encouraged dialogues about the events of the Stolen Generations, several conservative journalists and historians did not want to accept important research that is relevant to
20 the Stolen Generations.

Luckily not all Australians are afraid of discussing racism and prejudice. To begin with, many people have reacted with a strong feeling of moral responsibility for the survivors of the Stolen Generations. They criticize the government for discriminating against the Aborigines and destroying Aboriginal culture. They declare that mixed-race children who
25 were born during this period have grown up without recognition altogether. Since the government has not given them enough opportunities to become successful human beings, many now live a life of segregation. Many Australians have commented on the unfair political disadvantages the Aborigines experience, and some are extremely determined to do something about it. The film industry has produced blockbuster films on the Stolen
30 Generations and writers have written books that openly debate the poor moral standards of society. People do not speak out of pity for the Stolen Generations. Instead, they speak up because they are dedicated to truth and honour.

Today, survivors of the Stolen Generations are still working hard to find their families and rebuild their lives. As a survivor of the Stolen Generations, you will not be able to forget
35 the trauma and sadness of your past easily. However, your friends and family give you strength to go on fighting for your cause. What we see on the faces of the Stolen Generations today is the Aboriginal strength that will not stay silent or give up.

1 Unit

Now complete the sentences below with suitable information from the text.

1 For more than 60 years during the 20th century, the Australian government _____

_____ .

2 The government made the children _____

and _____ .

3 When people speak about the Stolen Generations, they mean _____

_____ .

4 Even today, many mixed-race children live a life full of disadvantages because _____

_____ .

5 However, many Australians support the survivors of the Stolen Generations _____

_____ .

6 Although Aborigines still suffer from their past, _____

_____ .   **More help** ➜ *(p. 54/–3 Punkte)*

2 WORDS In English, please!   / 7

Was sagst du, wenn du sagen willst, …

1 … dass du jemandem leider nicht helfen kannst? _____

_____

2 … dass du außer Sydney noch eine Küstenregion besuchen möchtest? _____

_____ .

3 … dass jemand ehrlich zu dir sein soll? _____

_____

4 … dass du einerseits Australien gern besuchen würdest, du andererseits aber weißt, dass der Flug dahin sehr

lange dauert? _____ .

5 … dass es gestern den ganzen Tag bewölkt war und schließlich zu regnen anfing? _____

_____

6 … dass du entschlossen bist, mit 18 Jahren nach Australien zu reisen? _____

_____ .

7 … dass du bedauerst, dass du in diesem Punkt völlig anderer Meinung bist als dein Gesprächspartner?

_____

Unit 1

3 WORDS What an interesting country! /14

Imagine you are an exchange student in Australia and would like to travel around a bit. So you read articles and take notes on interesting places. When you finally want to start planning your journey, you notice that you cannot read all the words because some water has dropped onto the paper. Look at the text and fill in the missing words and phrases.

Lots of different landscapes:

1 Far North Queensland is a _____ area in the north-east of Australia. In the wet season,

there can be a lot of rain and roads can be _____ and the climate can be very

_____. I should go along the _____ coastal route to see the

largest _____ in the world. Maybe I could even _____ there

in the sea to see all the beautiful fish! But I should be aware of salties. This kind of

_____ sometimes swims out from the river into the sea!

2 Go _____ into the outback? It is a vast, flat, _____ area

with some _____ towns and villages. I'd love to learn more about the native people and

their _____ culture. And maybe I will also see _____ – they

are animals typical of Australia and only live there.

3 Things to take with me: _____ to protect me from the sun, a torch to find my way

at night and a map of the _____ to know where I have to go.

7

1 Unit

4 LANGUAGE Port Augusta and the world's longest mail run / 5

As a reporter for your English school magazine, you write a text on Australia.
You have found a lot of information and want to make the text more interesting.
Rewrite the sentences using participle clauses.

1 In the middle of the 19th century, supplies which were taken to Australia's outback from Port Augusta had to be carried by camels because they were the only animals which could survive in this dry land.

2 Railway tracks which were built in the early 1900s connected the south with Alice Springs or Perth and were the most reliable and fastest way of transport.

3 The electricity which is produced in Augusta's large power station today is mostly used in Adelaide, 300 km away.

4 Every Saturday lots of mail and a maximum of three people that are carried by an airplane take off at Port Augusta on the South Australian coast.

5 The pilot who is sent out to remote villages and towns to deliver and pick up mail flies across the vast inland area of the bush.

8

Unit 1

5 LANGUAGE A day in Sydney / 9

Another text in your English school magazine is about a day in Sydney.
You would like to add some pictures with captions.

First match the sentence beginnings with the pictures. Then finish each sentence with a participle clause.

A

B

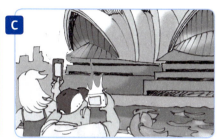
C

D

E

F

1 [C] People on the boat _taking photos of the opera house_.
2 [A] In the Rocks people sat in a café _drinking sth_.
3 [F] Children walk along the beach _eating an ice-cream_.
4 [E] Everyone stood in the Royal Botanic Gardens _looking at the animals_.
5 [D] A woman enjoys a day out _watching a singer on the street_.
6 [B] A man sits in a quiet place _reading a book_.

6 SPEAKING A visit to Australia / 15

01 Imagine you are an exchange student in Australia. At the moment you are in Sydney where you meet a group of teenagers. They are really interested in Germany and ask you lots of questions. One of them also tells you why he would like to visit Germany.

Listen to his talk. While listening you can take notes, for example on the structure of the text or on linking words. This can help you to prepare your own talk.

Now he would like to know why you wanted to visit Australia. Give your answer in a two-minute talk. The pictures might give you some ideas. You can make notes to structure your ideas before you start speaking.

1 Unit

7 MEDIATION A visit to Australia /12

As an exchange student you read the story of Adam Goodes in your social studies class.
Your teacher has asked you to think of something you can do against racism.
Together with some of your classmates you collect ideas for a project.

You search the internet for information and find the following article:

www.toleranz-weltweit.de

16. November –
Internationaler Tag der Toleranz

Jeder Mensch ist gleich viel wert, obwohl doch jeder anders ist!

Unter diesem Motto organisieren viele Schulen einen Tag, der ganz im Zeichen der Akzeptanz Anderer steht. Dabei ist es nicht bedeutsam, ob es um Menschen aus anderen Kulturen, Menschen mit Behinderung oder Menschen mit anderen Ansichten geht. Wichtig ist, dass jeder den Wunsch hat, so akzeptiert zu werden, wie er ist und dass das nur geht, wenn man Andere toleriert und respektiert.

Daher können die Schüler selbst organisieren, was sie an diesem Tag machen wollen:
Die Sportler veranstalten einen Lauf und spenden das Geld für jede gelaufene Runde[1] einer Organisation, z. B. Unicef.

Außerdem spielen zwei „bunte" Fußballmannschaften gegeneinander, das heißt, die Fußballer kommen aus verschiedenen Ländern und sprechen verschiedene Muttersprachen. Die meisten lernen Deutsch, sodass sie sich gut verständigen können. Wenn es doch einmal an einem Wort fehlt, weichen sie auf Englisch aus.

Ein Team organisiert ein „buntes" Buffet. Gerichte aus verschiedenen Ländern werden zubereitet und anschließend gemeinsam verzehrt.

Gibt es eine bessere Gelegenheit, als dabei der Musik anderer Kulturen zu lauschen? Wohl nicht und genau aus diesem Grund hat sich eine Band gebildet und einige Kinder singen Lieder aus ihrem Heimatland. Natürlich darf dazu auch getanzt werden. Außerdem diskutieren und debattieren Gäste und Schüler zum Thema Rassismus, ein Thema, das einfach jeden etwas angeht.

Das wichtigste an diesem Tag ist, dass nicht nur über die betroffenen Menschen geredet wird, sondern dass sie selbst dabei sind und alle das Miteinander gestalten.

Report back to your fellow students on the main ideas of the article.

You can write down your text or record yourself when you speak.

[1] Runde = lap

Unit 1

Klassenarbeit B

Gesamtpunktzahl ▢ / 85

1 LISTENING A radio show: people in the outback 🎧

/ 29

02 The host of the radio show welcomes different people to the programme and talks to them about living and working in the outback.

a) Listen to the first part of the radio show and tick (✔) the correct answers.
Be careful: sometimes more than one answer is correct.

/ 9

1 The School of the Air

  a) is a school for students all over Australia. ◯

  b) was founded to teach children in the outback. ◯

  c) has made education available in remote areas for more than 60 years. ◯

  d) is a school on an airplane. ◯

2 When children have classes

  a) they are somewhere at home. ◯

  b) they go to Alice Springs. ◯

  c) teachers and other students most often talk to each other through satellite radios. ◯

  d) one of their parents is the teacher. ◯

3 Philip White

  a) and his friend Marka are of the same age and have classes together. ◯

  b) has always lived in the Northern Territories with his family. ◯

  c) is an Aboriginal student. ◯

  d) has classes with the School of the Air at Marka's home. ◯

4 The School of the Air can only be successful because

  a) students and teachers can use very good communication technology. ◯

  b) classes are taught through television. ◯

  c) the speed of the internet is as fast as in cities. ◯

  d) teachers can connect to the students through telephone or satellite radio. ◯

5 Students at the School of the Air

  a) never meet their teacher in person. ◯

  b) usually meet their classmates once a year in Alice Springs. ◯

  c) are all in Australia. ◯

  d) are regularly visited at home by their teacher. ◯

11

1 Unit

b) 🔊 03 Now listen to the second part of the programme and tick (✓) the things they talk about. /5

The host of the radio show, Michelle Smith, and her guest, Dr Catherine Emangu, talk about

1 how people live and work in the outback. ◯
2 how Ms Emangu was trained as a doctor at university. ◯
3 a service offering help to people who live far away from cities. ◯
4 the different medical services people in the outback and in the cities need. ◯
5 when and how the Royal Flying Doctor Service started. ◯
6 how the Royal Flying Doctor Service is organized. ◯
7 which different services the Royal Flying Doctor Service offers. ◯
8 the fact that their service is limited to the people in the outback. ◯

c) 🔊 03 Now listen again to the second part of the programme and complete the following beginnings of sentences with information given in the show. You can listen to the recording twice. /15

1 This part of the radio show is about how _____ in an emergency.

2 As a doctor with the Royal Flying Doctor Service (RFDS), Catherine Emangu helps _____ when they _____ .

3 At the beginning of the 20th century, Reverend John Flynn _____ and decided to use it to start the RFDS because a lot of people in rural areas _____ .

4 These days the RFDS flies _____ from _____ and helps _____ .

5 The RFDS offers services such as _____ . (3 items)

6 In general, the doctors of the RFDS do not only _____ , but also _____ in an emergency situation.

7 To give an example, Dr. Emangu speaks about a woman who _____ because _____ .

12

Unit 1

2 WORDS Preparing a barbecue   / 9

Phil and Susan talk about having a barbecue in the evening.
Use the words and phrases from the box to complete the sentences. There are more words than you need.

> way · afraid · honest · opportunity · very first · talkative · have a point ·
> totally · firstly · in the end · unfortunately · possibility · secondly

Phil: Should we prepare a barbie tonight in our garden?

Susan: Brilliant idea! That would be a good _____ for our exchange student

Martin to meet some of our friends.

Phil: Right. To start with, we should think about food.

Susan: Sorry, I _____ disagree here: _____, we should check

the weather forecast. There is always a _____ of rain in Sydney in May.

Phil: You _____ there, but I already have and found out that the weather will be fine.

Susan: Well, having settled that we should, _____, come back to the food.

Let's buy some beef and …

Phil: … oh, I'm _____ Martin is vegetarian, so we should have some vegetables, too.

Susan: That's true, _____ I didn't know that. Well, it isn't a problem,

we will have a mix of food then.

Phil: Is it Martin's _____ time enjoying an Aussie barbie?

Susan: Well, I don't know. Let's find out then. We'll have fun!

3 WORDS Opposites   / 9

Find the opposites to the following words.

1 dry   ◄ ► _____

2 rural   ◄ ► _____

3 boring   ◄ ► _____

4 (to) support something ◄ ► _____

5 public   ◄ ► _____

6 quiet   ◄ ► _____

7 shy   ◄ ► _____

8 strict   ◄ ► _____

9 unfair   ◄ ► _____

1 Unit

4 WORDS Aspects of Australia /9

Find the word that fits the context and fill it in the grid. The letters in the blue boxes form a word that describes types of snakes that live in Australia.

1 In the ▢ rainforest of Australia there are many huge trees, bushes and lots of animals.
2 Most Australian inhabitants live along the eastern ▢.
3 The native people of Australia are called ▢.
4 When you visit the continent, you should protect your skin with ▢.
5 The central area of the country is referred to as the bush or the ▢.
6 The Opera House is a very famous Sydney ▢.
7 A saltie is a type of ▢.
8 Some parts get a lot of rain and the temperatures are very high, so the area is rather ▢.
9 Woolloomooloo with its wharf is a trendy ▢ part of Sydney.

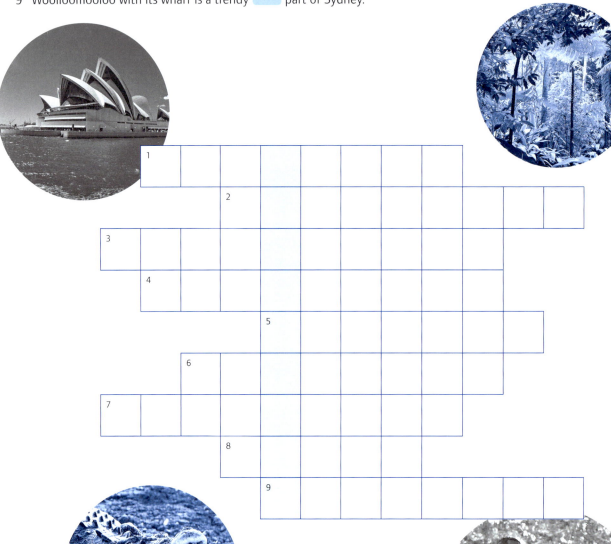

→ Lösungswort: _____

Unit 1

5 LANGUAGE Aboriginal people in Australia   / 7

Use participle clauses to join the sentences that match best. Use when or while in the
participle clause. Sometimes you have to change the sentence from the left side of the table
into a participle clause, sometimes the sentence from the right.

0	Aboriginal people made their way from Africa to Australia.	Aboriginal people lived from hunting and farming.
1	Aboriginal people lived on the same lands.	Aboriginal people spoke many different languages or dialects.
2	Aboriginal people walked across the land.	Aboriginal people sang songlines to describe their ways.
3	Aboriginal people used a special melody or rhythm.	Aboriginal people talked about landmarks so that they could find their way.
4	British colonists built towns in coastal regions.	British colonists arrived in Australia at the end of the 18th century.
5	Aboriginal people were forced to work for the Europeans.	Aboriginal people were not recognized as citizens.
6	For about 70 years the government discriminated against the native people.	The government made the Aborigines live in institutions and speak English.
7	The Australian parliament apologized to the Stolen Generations in 2008.	The Australian parliament started its support to keep the Aboriginal culture alive today.

0 *Aboriginal people lived from hunting and farming when making their way from Africa to Australia.*

1 _____

_____

2 _____

_____

3 _____

_____

4 _____

_____

5 _____

_____

6 _____

_____

7 _____

_____

1 Unit

6 LANGUAGE   At the beach in Far North Queensland   /7

Imagine you walk along the beach in Far North Queensland. When looking around you notice different things. Have a look at the pictures. Then use the verbs to make sentences with participle clauses.

0 watch – film

1 hear – arrive

2 spot – swim

3 smell – roast

4 see – run

5 notice – read

6 listen to – play

7 feel – land

0 I watched a man filming his two little children on the sand.

1 I heared a boat coming
2 I spotted a women swimming
3 I smelt sb. roasting a beef
4 I saw a bird running to 2 people
5 I noticed a men reading a book
6 I listened to a person playing piano
7 I felt a raindrop landing on my nose

Unit 1

7 WRITING Would I like to go to the School of the Air? ✎ / 15

On the radio show you have heard about Philip White who attends the School of the Air in Australia. This concept sounds very interesting to you, so you start thinking about advantages and disadvantages of this type of school. Brainstorm ideas for and against the School of the Air and put them in a table.

For	Against

Now share your ideas with Philip and write an email to him. Point out advantages and disadvantages of the School of the Air. Follow the steps for writing an argumentative text on page 17 of your student's book. Write about 150 to 180 words.

More help ➔ *(p. 54/–3 Punkte)*

To: philip.white@australiamail.au

Subject: Attending the School of the Air

17

2 Unit

Relationships

Mein Lernplan

Datum

Was kommt dran?

| Datum | Was ich lernen will | Erledigt? | Was ich noch einmal wiederholen muss/wichtige Hinweise |

| | Unit | 2 |

Klassenarbeit A

Gesamtpunktzahl [ ] / 67

1 LISTENING A radio programme on the science of twins 🎧 /14

04 Martin Richmond welcomes Dr. Julie Riley and Anthony Carter on his weekly radio show.

a) Listen to the radio programme and tick (✔) which statement best expresses
what the conversation is about. /1

1 Julie Riley and Anthony Carter talk about the relationship between human beings,
especially the one between twins. ◯

2 The scientist and the caller agree on the fact that the relationship between twins
and the one between brothers and sisters are the same. ◯

3 The guests on the radio programme argue about how relationships between people develop. ◯

b) Look at the following statements and decide in which order the speakers
of the radio programme mention them. /6

1 ◯ The family members in Tony's family have a very close relationship to each other.

2 ◯ Even if twins do not grow up in the same family, they might lead very similar lives as adults.

3 ◯ Anthony Carter describes his relationship with his sister when they were younger.

4 ◯ Ms Riley points out that the basis of the relationship of twins is both their similar DNA
and the time they share before they are born.

5 ◯ After a short break, the host of the show welcomes his two guests back to the programme.

6 ◯ Even though the connection between twins is already amazing, the one of identical twins
is even more fascinating and special.

c) Listen again and tick (✔) which of the guests on the radio show says what. /7

	The scientist Dr. Julie Riley	The caller Anthony Carter
1 The relationship between brothers and sisters can be very close, no matter whether they are twins or not.	◯	◯
2 Brothers and sisters develop a close relationship when growing up together and by being interested in each other.	◯	◯
3 Twins are different to brothers and sisters since they might experience the same things in life without knowing each other.	◯	◯
4 The majority of twins lead a normal life and have their own personalities.	◯	◯
5 Twins develop such a close connection before they are born.	◯	◯
6 It is really special that very close family members can feel the same even though they are not in the same place.	◯	◯

19

2 Unit

2 WORDS An email to a counselling helpline   / 11

Complete Megan's email to the counselling helpline of the website *www.allaboutteens.co.uk*
for young people with suitable words from the box. There are more words than you need.
Sometimes you have to change the form of the word.

> (to) be attracted to · (to) fall in love with · (to) date ·
> be seeing · (to) break up · annoyed with ·
> confused · cross · frightened · hopeful · pleased · heartbroken ·
> thrilled · terrified · (to) get to know

To: counseller@allaboutteens.co.uk

Subject: My boyfriend

Dear Counsellor,

My name is Megan and I am 15 years old. At the moment, I'm very _____

and _____! Let me tell you why: I've _____ this really nice

and good-looking boy for two months.

We _____ each other when he was new in my class at the beginning

of the school year. He was friendly and talkative and I liked it very much when he was around. And I

_____ his blue eyes and his nice smile. You can imagine that I was

_____ when he first asked me out to the cinema. This was when he started to

_____ me. Of course, we met at school each day. Being together after school is much

different though: we spent time outside, just talking and enjoying the time together. We prepared little

surprise presents for each other. So I was really happy and _____ with the situation.

Then one day we wanted to meet in front of a café, but he was late. I was a bit _____

with him, but he apologized. When he was late the next two times, I was really _____

with him, but he didn't want to talk about it. And yesterday he suddenly told me that he wants to

_____ with me. I don't understand this!

Can you help me, please? Please tell me what I should do.

Best, Megan

20

Unit 2

3 WORDS Talking about what you eat
/ 8

Find the word or phrase that fits the context best.

1 All the things you normally eat every day, every week are your _____ .

2 The opposite of sick or ill: _____ .

3 A lot of children say it is their favourite food for lunch. They often eat it with tomato sauce: _____ .

4 Some people say we _____ stop eating meat

   to give the food to hungry people, not animals.

5 Vegetarians must be careful to get enough _____ , for example from tofu.

6 Food like milk, butter, cheese or meat should be kept in the _____ to keep it fresh.

7 Eating soup or fish for lunch on Fridays used to be a _____ in many families.

8 If you like something sweet, enjoy _____ chocolate –

   it's more expensive than the ones from factories, but much more delicious.

4 LANGUAGE What would have happened?
/ 12

Imagine these things happened last week. Write sentences about what would have happened
or what you would have done.

1 If I _____ (not – miss) the bus last Monday morning,

   I _____ (not – be) late for school.

2 My English test last Tuesday _____ (be) much better,

   if I _____ (study) a bit every day instead of everything on the day before.

3 I _____ (not – tear) my jeans

   if I _____ (not – climb) the tree behind our house last Wednesday.

4 If I _____ (not – leave) my telephone at home last Thursday,

   I _____ (text) my mother that I would be home late.

5 My brother will be 18 tomorrow. He _____ (vote) in last Sunday's elections,

   if he _____ (be) 18 by then.

6 If I _____ (not – have) a cold last weekend,

   _____ (go) out with my friends.

21

2 Unit

5 LANGUAGE Giving advice   / 7

Look at the pictures and complete the sentences with **be supposed to** or **had better**.

You _____ (leave) your bike at the fence.

You _____ (park) it

in the bicycle parking area behind the school.

Teacher: It's already 9 o'clock. _____

you _____ (be) in class right now?

Student: Yes, sir. I'm sorry, my bus was late.

Teacher: So you _____ (hurry)

now to get to your room.

Father: Mum will be home by 6 o'clock – so we _____

_____ (prepare) dinner now.

Then we can eat together and talk about what we've done today.

Son: Alright, let's get started.

I have a difficult exam tomorrow, so I _____

_____ (stop) chatting with my friends now and go to bed.

According to the advert, the film _____

_____ (start) at 8 o'clock in the cinema.

6 WRITING An everyday hero ✏   / 15

You have seen the following advert in an international youth magazine for schools
and would like to participate. Read the advert and write a text of about 150 to 200 words.

> Write an article about a person of everyday life who impressed you very much.
> It could be someone you know personally or you have heard of or read about.
> We will publish the best articles in next month's edition.

22

| Unit | **2** |

Klassenarbeit B

Gesamtpunktzahl ☐ / 74

1 READING Coast to coast (from the novel by David Fermer) 📖 / 15

Cooper Jackson, a 17-year-old Australian boy, discovers an Afghan boy at the beach and decides to help him by hiding him in a hut near the beach. He goes there every day after school to give the boy clean clothes and food. Cooper only tells his classmate Kate about this, but it is a step too far for her to help an illegal immigrant. Read the excerpt from the novel.

After school I went home to get more food. No one was there so I could move around the house freely. I grabbed a sports bag from my room and filled it with stuff from the kitchen, careful only to take so
5 much that nobody would notice: half a packet of my sister's cereals, a can of pineapple chunks, some more biscuits, nothing that anyone would miss.

I was just about to leave when Dad's voice hit me out of the blue: "Hi, Coop!"
10 I spun around, eyes wide like the thief caught red-handed who I was. Dad was leaning against the doorframe, his tie loose around his neck. He was home earlier than I expected.

"You were out late last night," he said in a voice
15 that sounded like it was trying to be friendly. "Where were you?"

I had no choice but to lie, and years of experience have taught me that a lie which tells the truth is always the better lie.
20 "Down at the beach," I said.

"With Graham?"

I hesitated. "No. Alone."

Dad stepped into the kitchen and looked at the bag. "What's that?"
25 "I'm going around to Kate's to do some project work," I said, thinking on my feet. Kate is always my best alibi. Dad loves her.

"And Kate needs bananas?"

I looked at the bag. A bunch of bananas was
30 sticking out of the open zip.

"The project is all about … bananas," I said.

Dad laughed as if he could see straight through me but for some reason didn't care. He wanted to avoid an argument, that much was clear.
35 "Do you want a drink?" he asked, going to the fridge.

"Na, I'm fine, thanks." I pushed the bananas back into the bag, zipped it up and checked my watch. It was gone four. I was running late.

"Listen, Coop," Dad said, taking out a soda. "You
40 and I haven't been getting along too well recently. I think it's time we talked."

Not now, Dad! Please! I really don't need this right now.

"It's no big deal," I said, throwing the bag over my
45 shoulder. I thought if I gave him a convincing display of indifference, Dad would let it go.

"Well it is to me," Dad insisted. "You're important, son, and I want us to get along."

He put his hand on my shoulder. It felt strange –
50 familiar and far away at the same time. I couldn't remember the last time he touched me.

"I know this campaign is difficult for you," he continued. "It's difficult for all of us. For your mom, for your sister, for me."
55 I had planned to take some milk, but I decided to leave that now. All I wanted was for Dad to stop talking.

"I've gotta go, Dad."

I took a step past him, heading for the door, but Dad held me back. "Wait a sec! You can't just leave!"
60 I can't?

"Family is important, Coop. It's the most important thing in the world. Don't you want us to get along?"

"We would get along a lot better if you just let me go."
65 Dad held onto my arm. He looked at the bag, then back to me, and forced a smile onto his face. An act of mind over matter.

"All right, Coop," he said, his voice softer. He let go of my arm. "You go if you have to, mate. I don't want
70 to hold you up." I took a step to the door. He was trying to sound casual again. "Maybe you and I can go fishing some time, what d'you say? Just like old times. You and me. A boy's day out I bet there are plenty of fish out there this time of year. We could –"
75 I didn't hear his last words. I was out of the kitchen and hurrying down the hall. I didn't look back. Out the front door. Down the steps. Along the drive. I couldn't believe my luck. I had taken a bag full of food without Dad even asking me what I was doing with
80 it! Bananas for Kate? Yeah, mate! And kangaroos do karate!

"Hey, Coop!" Dad's voice rang out again. I slipped out of the front gate and turned to close it. Dad was standing on the porch. "I love you, son!" he called
85 out, and his words stabbed me like a knife. "You take care of yourself!"

23

2 Unit

a) Decide which of the short summaries best describes what happens in the excerpt. /1

1 Cooper packs a bag with food to sleep at his friend Kate's house,
  but his father doesn't allow him to go. ◯

2 Cooper wants to leave the house as soon as possible with a sports bag full of food,
  but his father wants to talk to him about their relationship. ◯

3 Cooper is angry with his dad because his dad wants to talk to him about their relationship
  when Cooper has no time. He accepts his father's suggestion to go fishing some time and talk then. ◯

b) The following statements describe Cooper's relationship with his father.
   Find quotes in the text to give proof. Add the lines too. /6

1 The relationship between father and son doesn't seem to be too good.
  They don't seem to get along well with each other.

_____

_____

_____

2 Cooper seems to be used to lying.

_____

_____

_____

3 He seems to be doing things his parents aren't supposed to know about.

_____

_____

_____

c) Now add more aspects to describe Cooper's relationship with his father.
   Find quotes in the text to give proof, too, and also add the lines. /6

_____

_____

_____

_____

_____

_____

More help ➡ (p. 54/–3 Punkte)

d) Explain the following lines: "I love you, son!" he called out, and his words stabbed me like a knife.
   "You take care of yourself!". Write your answer in your exercise book. /2

24

Unit 2

2 WORDS Social networks   /11

Two students meet at break time and talk to each other about their classes. Read their dialogue and complete it with the missing words from the box. There are more words than you need.

> communication · useful · percentage · amount of · absolutely · account · enter · acquaintance · be supposed to · occasionally · anyway · serious · distant · pretty · update

Thomas: Imagine, today I was allowed to use my mobile phone in my English class. I thought we _____ switch it off all day at school.

Lucy: That's right. However, I had to use it _____ in my French class, too.

Thomas: What did you do?

Lucy: Well, our teacher wanted us to talk to our partner class in France. So our mobile phones were really _____ to contact them. Hannah, you know, often chats with her French partner student Pauline. That's why I'd say she is not just an _____, but a real friend.

Thomas: _____! Sounds _____ cool.

Lucy: What did you do with your mobile phone in your English class?

Thomas: We studied vocabulary with an app. I couldn't start right away, because I first had to _____ it. The _____ time we worked with it was a lot. But _____, I didn't like it.

Lucy: What would you have liked to do?

Thomas: I think I only want to use my mobile phone for _____ with my friends. At school, I prefer the computer: we can access our personal _____, use the internet to find information or work on project material.

Lucy: Well, I completely agree with you. – Time for PE now – see you later.

Thomas: See you.

25

2 Unit

3 LANGUAGE Do you think you could …?   / 6

Imagine you are an exchange student and have to ask different people about different things.
Look at the people in the pictures and think about who wants to ask who to do what.
First imagine the people are good friends, then imagine they are strangers.
Write down the requests in different ways.

> **!** The box "Access to cultures" on p. 41 in your textbook might help you to use good phrases.

The people are good friends and say:

1 _____

2 _____

3 _____

The people are strangers and say:

1 _____

2 _____

3 _____

More help ➔ (p. 54/–3 Punkte)

26

Unit 2

4 LANGUAGE What should we do?   / 12

Your friend Lara spends time with her friend Lauren in England.
Look at the following situations and decide what the girls could say.
Complete the dialogues using should, ought to, be supposed to, be said to and had better.

Lauren: I think, you _____ try fish 'n chips,

it _____ to be the most famous English dish.

Lara: I'm afraid that's not a good idea, because I'm a vegetarian and

don't like fish. I _____ have some vegetables or a salad.

Lara: I'd love to see London from above.

Lauren: No problem, then we _____ take a ride

on the London Eye. We'll have a fantastic view from the top.

Lara: _____ we try to get tickets for a musical?

Lauren: Brilliant idea, let's try to buy tickets at the box office over there.

Lara: Can you see the sign: "Sold out".

Lauren: What a pity! We _____ buy tickets in

advance next time.

Lauren: Let's go to the cinema instead.

Lara: We _____ find out what's on first

and then decide.

Lauren: I'm sorry, you _____ use your mobile

in the cinema. I think you _____

turn it off.

Lauren: We _____ be home by 10 pm.

Lara: We _____ not be late, otherwise your mum

will be worried.

Lauren: That's right. So we _____ take the tube now.

27

Unit 2

5 MEDIATION Building bridges! 🇬🇧 /15

🔊 05 Your English partner school organizes the project Building bridges! They want to bring people of different nationalities closer together. That's why the organization team is looking for ideas and asks you to report on projects that you know about at your school or in your area. You hear the following podcast on the local radio and think it introduces a good idea.

Listen to the podcast "Das Chemnitzer Filmfestival SCHLINGEL" and report the relevant information for the Building Bridges! project.

6 SPEAKING Talking about statistics – using the internet 💬 /15

🔊 06 You are taking part in a project that Year 9 students at your school do with their partner school. The topic of the project is the use of electronic devices and the internet, especially among young people.

Matthew, a student from your partner school, talks to you on Skype about their results and asks you to tell him something about your findings on German users.

Listen to Matthew first.

NOW YOU
In order to answer Matthew's questions, have a look at the statistics about young people in Germany using electronic devices and the internet and prepare a short talk of about two minutes.

> ❗ You can use Skills File 26 on p. 157 of your student's book to prepare your talk and Skills File 27 on p. 158 to give yourself feedback on your talk.

How often do people in general use the internet?		
2006	2010	2016
65 %	75 %	84 %

Source: https://www.destatis.de/DE/ZahlenFakten/GesellschaftStaat/EinkommenKonsumLebensbedingungen/ITNutzung/Tabellen/ZeitvergleichComputernutzung_IKT.html

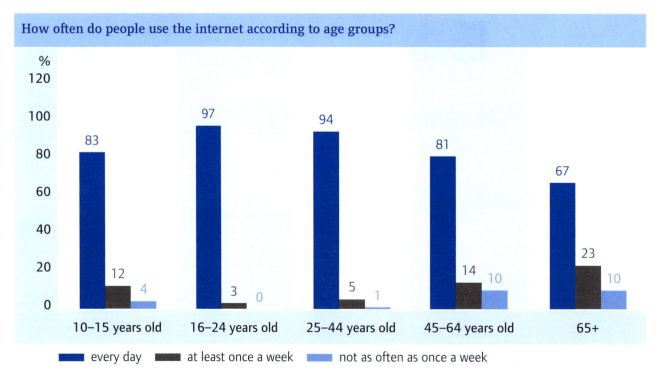

Source: https://www.destatis.de/DE/ZahlenFakten/GesellschaftStaat/EinkommenKonsumLebensbedingungen/ITNutzung/Tabellen/NutzungInternetAlter_IKT.html

Unit 2

What do young people between 12 and 25 use the internet for?

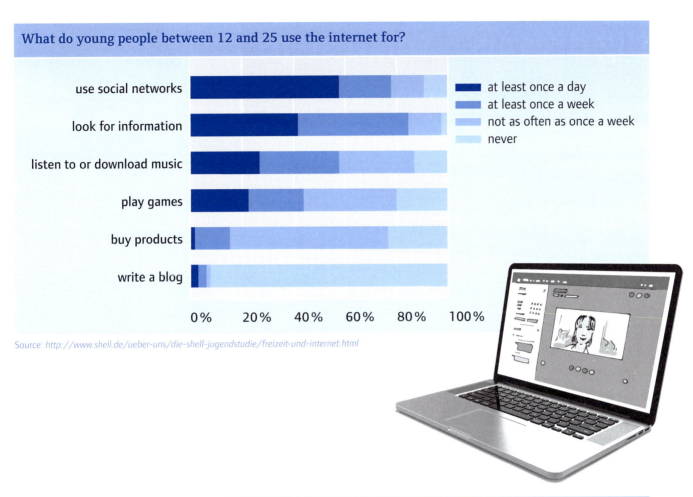

Source: http://www.shell.de/ueber-uns/die-shell-jugendstudie/freizeit-und-internet.html

What do students do most often with their smartphones?

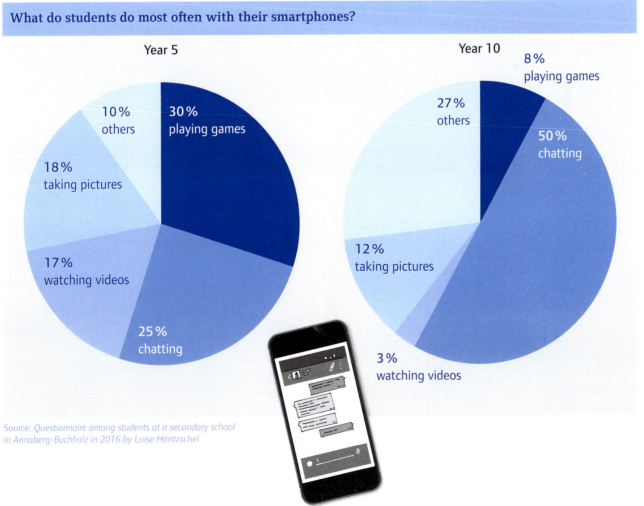

Source: Questionnaire among students at a secondary school in Annaberg-Buchholz in 2016 by Luise Häntzschel

3 Unit

Big dreams – small steps

Mein Lernplan

Datum

Was kommt dran?

Datum	Was ich lernen will	Erledigt?	Was ich noch einmal wiederholen muss/wichtige Hinweise

Unit 3

Klassenarbeit A

Gesamtpunktzahl ____ /80

1 READING Young people protect our environment ▢ /9

Read the following article that you found in a school magazine.

The Salisbury High Gazette   Issue 6, Volume 29

Help! – Planet in trouble

We are not the most responsible generation on this planet. Every minute that we leave the lights on in our classrooms and homes or have the water running on full speed, we are damaging our planet.
5 Although everybody's actions have an impact on the environment, a lot of people still act irresponsibly. We know we must recycle, reuse and reduce. Yet we are not doing it.

Our research team interviewed students and teachers
10 at this school. They learned that more than 80 % of our students and teachers buy bottled water every day. But there are water fountains[1] on every level of the school building! 96 % of those interviewed said they use more than 3 pieces of paper whenever
15 they wash their hands. But every toilet has an electric hand dryer! Today, more than any other time in history, we need to ask ourselves a very important question. "What can we do as a school community to make our planet greener?"

20 Let's start with reducing[2] and recycling our natural resources[3]. We don't need to keep the lights on in our classrooms when we have natural light outside. In a school in Malta, students from the age of 5 to 11 have become 'watchdogs'. They take turns to
25 walk around the school asking people to turn off the classroom lights. They also check that the taps in the toilets are properly turned off. One of their jobs is to work with the canteen manager every Wednesday to make sure that they have low-meat
30 and high-vegetable school lunches every day. At the moment, these active students are working closely with their friends and teachers on a new school-wide recycling project called the 'Newspaper Recycling Campaign'.

35 Our magazine team has formed a group at our school called 'Friends of the Environment'. We are looking for students and teachers who are interested in making our planet a better place to join our team. Our job is to set rules for energy saving and to make
40 regular checks to see if there are any improvements to our policies. In fact, we have already started discussions with our principal about the possibility of installing solar panels[4], and we are happy to report that she is just as excited as we are about doing
45 our part to save the environment. We are hoping to be able to reduce our total energy consumption[5] by 20 % at the end of this school year. If you are interested in joining our team, please meet us at the magazine office in G2.15 next Monday between
50 9:30 and 10:30.

Imagine a school where everyone works together to save the planet, even before the school day begins. Our interviews show that over 75 % of our students and teachers live within 5 km to 8 km of the school.
55 Unfortunately, less than 25 % of them walk or cycle to school. Over 80 % students and teachers prefer to travel to school by car, regardless of where they live. We need to ask what kind of planet we want to leave our children and grandchildren. Do we want
60 them to suffer[6] strong weather conditions and increasing temperatures? For a start, we would like to win our principal over to declare Mondays, Wednesdays and Thursdays as 'Cycle-to-School Days' and offer prizes to students and teachers who cycle
65 to school on all of those days for at least 3 months. If we see good results at our small school, we would like to meet with our town's mayor. Together as a whole community, we could play a bigger role in saving our planet. So please join us!

---

[1]water fountain *place where you can drink water from a tap*   [2](to) reduce *make smaller in amount*
[3]natural resources *materials like wood, coal or water*   [4]solar panel *thing that produces energy by using the sun*
[5]consumption *use*   [6](to) suffer something *etwas erleiden*

3 | **Unit**

a) Now decide whether these statements are true or false. /6

	true	false
1 Every person is responsible for protecting the environment.	◯	◯
2 The majority of students and teachers prefer drinking water that is available in special places at school.	◯	◯
3 The Salisbury High Gazette team asks watchdogs to walk around school to save energy.	◯	◯
4 At the end of the school year, the total amount of energy used at the school will probably be smaller.	◯	◯
5 Three-quarters of the teachers and students walk or cycle to school.	◯	◯
6 The article asks students to join a team to take actions to save our planet.	◯	◯

b) Look at the wrong sentences again and correct them with information from the text. Write sentences. /3

Unit 3

2 WORDS Can you help me, please?   /11

Your cousin Megan has found an interesting advert and asks you for help.
Read her letter and complete the text with the missing words from the box.
There are more words than you need.

> (to) proofread • reverse • (to) matter • secondary •
> (to) apply for • primary • qualifications •
> date • curriculum vitae • applicant • personal • source •
> (to) include • (to) announce • application • knowledge

Dear Oliver,

I'm so excited. I found this advert of a summer job in England and would like to

_____ it. I think this will be a great opportunity to get to know the culture

better and increase my _____ about the country and its people,

don't you think?

I've already found out that I have to write a letter of _____ in which

I should probably _____ something about me and my skills and all my

_____ like languages and IT skills. They also ask me to write a

detailed _____. I'm not really sure how to do that and have lots of questions:

Do I have to start with a _____ statement? Do I have to speak about my

_____ and _____ school in _____

order? What else do I need to tell them?

May I ask you to help me, please? May I send you my documents and ask you to

_____ them? That would be fantastic!

Love,
Megan

33

3 Unit

3 WORDS In English, please
/ 20

Was sagst du, wenn du ausdrücken willst, …

1 … dass der letzte Termin für deine Bewerbung der nächste Freitag ist?

2 … dass es dir sehr peinlich ist, dass du den Geburtstag deines besten Freundes vergessen hast?

3 … dass jemand nicht schummeln soll?

4 … dass Joshua Humor hat?

5 … dass du, je eher du mit den Hausaufgaben anfängst, desto eher fertig sein wirst?

6 … dass wir rechtzeitig zum Abendbrot zu Hause sein könnten, wenn wir uns beeilen?

7 … dass die gegenwärtige Hitze eine Folge der Erderwärmung sein könnte?

8 … dass bisher niemand wirklich weiß, was die Erderwärmung auf lange Sicht stoppen könnte?

9 … dass weder deine Mutter noch dein Vater in einer großen Firma arbeiten.

10 … dass dein Bruder den Test nicht bestehen wird, wenn er nicht mehr dafür tut.

More help ➔ *(p. 55/–3 Punkte)*

Unit 3

4 LANGUAGE Plans and decisions /10

Choose the correct future form to complete the dialogues: will or going to.

1 **Aunt:** Have you got any plans what you want to do after leaving school?

   Niece: After graduating from college I _____ (do) work experience abroad.

2 **Kevin:** I'm on the way to the cinema. I _____ (watch) the film *Challenges*.

   Do you want to come with me?

   Phil: I'd love to, but I _____ (meet) my friend Lucy at a café in 10 minutes.

3 **Waiter:** What would you like to have for dinner – chicken or beef?

   Guest: I _____ (have) chicken, please.

4 **Traveller:** Do you know when the next bus to London leaves?

   Travel agent: Sorry, I don't, but I _____ (check) the timetable for you.

5 **Mum:** Have you heard the knock on the door?

   Hannah: No, I haven't. But I _____ (go) and have a look who it is. –

   It's Olivia, Mum. We _____ (study) for the English exam together.

6 **Son:** Tomorrow is Dad's birthday. Mum, have you got a present for him?

   Mum: I _____ (show) you what it is if you _____

   (not – tell) your father.

   Son: I _____ (not – say) anything, I promise.

5 MEDIATION My future career /15

🔊 07 You like horses very much and are a successful rider. You want to work as a
horse whisperer after finishing school.

You hear the following interview on the radio and use the information given on this career
to explain to your parents why horse whisperer will be the right job for you.

6 SPEAKING Useful information 💬 /15

🔊 08 Imagine you have applied for an exchange year programme to a British grammar school.
A teacher of this school wants to interview you on Skype. He sends you a set of questions
to prepare for the interview. Look at the set of questions and take notes.

− Can you tell me about yourself, please?
− What are your strengths and weaknesses?
− Why would you like to come to our school?
− What are your goals for this year at our school?
− Do you have any questions?

Now listen to the track online and conduct the interview.

35

3 Unit

Klassenarbeit B

Gesamtpunktzahl ___ / 65

1 LISTENING Interview on work experience 🎧 /8

🔊 09 Before you listen to the interview look at the following words and phrases:

- accounting [əˈkaʊntɪŋ] *Buchhaltung, Rechnungswesen*
- sales *(pl.)* [seɪlz] *Vertrieb*
- logistics department [ləd'ʒɪstɪks dɪˌpɑːtmənt] *Logistikabteilung*
- marketing department [ˈmɒrkətɪŋ dɪˌpɑːtmənt] *Vertriebsabteilung*
- administration department [ədˌmɪnɪˈstreɪʃn dɪˌpɑːtmənt] *Verwaltungsabteilung*
- law [lɔː] *Jura, Rechtswesen*
- lawyer [ˈlɔːjɜː] *Jurist/in, Anwalt/Anwältin*
- (to) accuse somebody [əkˈjuːz] *hier: jemanden anklagen*

Now listen to the short interview between Charles Bask, editor in chief of Career First Magazine and Ben Wright who is a Year 12 student at Rochester 6th Form College.

a) Decide which of the following statements describes the situation best and tick (✓) the answer. /1

1 The interviewer Charles Bask and the student Ben Wright agree in their interview that work experience at a big company is very important to start a successful career. ◯

2 The student Ben Wright gives tips in this interview for different students on how to apply for an interesting work experience. ◯

3 Charles Bask questions the student Ben Wright about the experience he and some of his fellow students gained during work experience at a big company. ◯

b) Now listen again and decide whether these statements are **true** or **false**. /7

		true	false
1	Not only Ben Wright, but all the students of his class, worked in different companies around Rochester.	◯	◯
2	Mr Grange was very helpful in arranging work experience for Ben's classmates.	◯	◯
3	Students at Rochester High School may do a three-week work experience which takes place just before the summer holidays.	◯	◯
4	Ben's friend Jacob didn't like the work in the factory because it was too noisy and hot.	◯	◯
5	Before her work experience, Rebecca wouldn't have liked to work in transportation.	◯	◯
6	Ben found out that even a car producing company needs to have a good law department.	◯	◯
7	Ben might go to university after having found out more about himself when travelling and working right after finishing school.	◯	◯

Unit 3

2 WORDS A crossword   / 13

Complete the sentences and fill in the crossword.

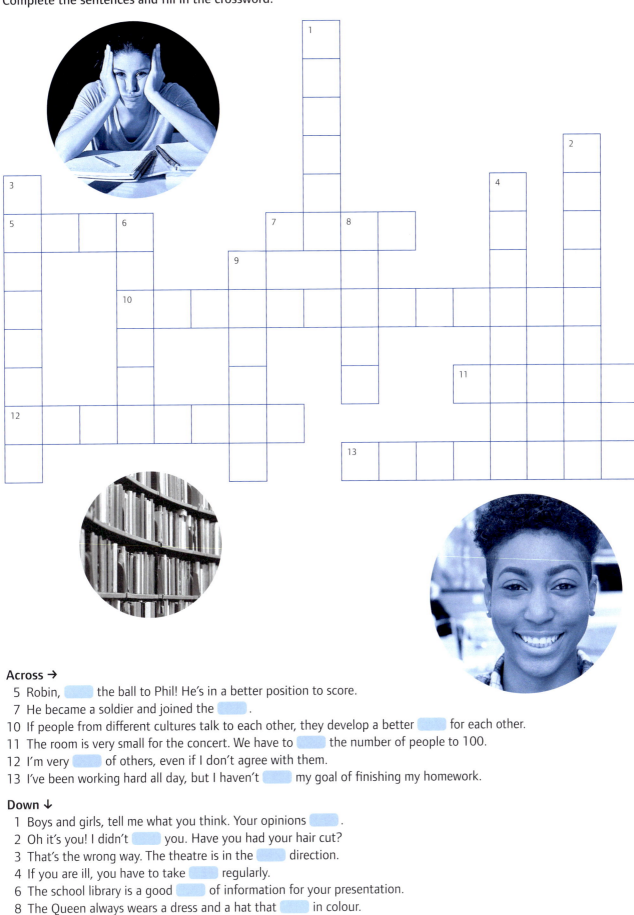

Across →
5 Robin, ⬚ the ball to Phil! He's in a better position to score.
7 He became a soldier and joined the ⬚.
10 If people from different cultures talk to each other, they develop a better ⬚ for each other.
11 The room is very small for the concert. We have to ⬚ the number of people to 100.
12 I'm very ⬚ of others, even if I don't agree with them.
13 I've been working hard all day, but I haven't ⬚ my goal of finishing my homework.

Down ↓
1 Boys and girls, tell me what you think. Your opinions ⬚.
2 Oh it's you! I didn't ⬚ you. Have you had your hair cut?
3 That's the wrong way. The theatre is in the ⬚ direction.
4 If you are ill, you have to take ⬚ regularly.
6 The school library is a good ⬚ of information for your presentation.
8 The Queen always wears a dress and a hat that ⬚ in colour.
9 Your skirt is much too short. You'd better wear a ⬚ dress if you go for a job interview.

37

Unit 3

3 LANGUAGE Just wait, I'll help you!   /10

Look at the pictures and complete the sentences.
Use the *will*-future or the present progressive for the verbs in brackets ( ).

! Wenn du unsicher bist, welche Zeitform du hier einsetzen musst, lies das Grammar File 1.5 auf S. 166–167 in deinem SB.

Unit 3

4 EXTRA LANGUAGE What would you advise me to do? /4

Look at the situations and say what you would do. Use have something done.

1 My bike is broken. –

 I think you should _____ (repair – bike shop).

2 The windows in your house always look perfect. –

 We _____ (clean) once a month.

3 I'm tired and often get headaches. –

 I think you should _____ (health – check) by a doctor.

4 What a nice dress! Did you sew it yourself? –

 No, I didn't. I _____ (make) by a friend of mine.

5 WRITING A letter of application /15

You found the following advert in a youth magazine. Read the advert first.
Then write a letter of application.

**Welcome to England –
exchange programmes for students**

Fish 'n chips, baked beans, plum pudding, scones and cream, marmalade – to name but a few delicious dishes England is famous for.

Get to know them, and much more when staying with an English host family.

Are you interested in improving your language skills?

English schools are quite different from German schools – so take up the challenge and become part of one of them for a limited time.

We offer 3-month/one-term, 6-month/two-term and 12-month/full year programmes.
Choose now and apply for your student exchange programme.

Send your letter of application and CV to:
John Best, The Best of England, 34 Prince Road, Wishwell H45 8JB, United Kingdom

! Das Skills File 10 auf S. 143 in deinem Schülerbuch hilft dir beim Verfassen eines Bewerbungsschreibens. Mithilfe des Bewertungsrasters auf S. 60 in diesem Heft kannst du deinen Entwurf überprüfen und überarbeiten.

Unit 3

6 MEDIATION Successful musicians   / 15

You are an excellent violin player and have been invited to an international summer school for students. The other participants, who come from all over the world, ask you about music competitions for young people in Germany.

They want to know:

- who can take part in these competitions
- where they take place
- whether you have to play a certain instrument
- who selects the pieces the participants play
- how the jury evaluates the candidates
- why people should take part in such competitions

a) First look at the following text, which gives information on such a competition – "Jugend musiziert". Read the text and mark up some keywords.

  Jugend musiziert

Wer den richtigen Ton trifft, ist nicht nur ein wortgewandter Redner in allen Situationen, sondern kann sich auch gute Chancen beim bundesweiten Musikwettbewerb *Jugend musiziert* für Schüler
5 und Jugendliche ausrechnen.

Jedes Jahr gibt es in allen Bundesländern Regional- und Landeswettbewerbe, bei denen Teilnehmerinnen und Teilnehmer ab der Grundschule bis zum 27. Lebensjahr ihr Können in verschiedenen
10 Kategorien unter Beweis stellen. Sowohl im Bereich „Instrument" als auch im „Gesang" können sie allein, mit einem Partner oder sogar im Orchester oder Chor ihr Talent präsentieren und sich mit anderen messen.

15 Dabei wechseln die Kategorien sowohl in den Regional- und Landeswettbewerben als auch im Bundeswettbewerb regelmäßig von Jahr zu Jahr leicht.

Teilnehmerinnen und Teilnehmer können zum
20 Beispiel in der Kategorie „Blechblasinstrumente" antreten, sich für die Teilnahme in der Kategorie „Klavier mit Begleitung Violine" entscheiden oder sie treten als „Vokalensemble" auf. Innerhalb dieser Kategorien werden verschiedene Alters-
25 gruppen unterschieden, sodass zum Beispiel die Neun- und Zehnjährigen oder die 16- und 17-Jährigen in einer Wertungsgruppe beurteilt werden. Die Teilnehmerinnen und Teilnehmer stellen sich ihr Programm für das Vorspiel selbst zusammen
30 und müssen dabei mit originalen Werken aus verschiedenen Epochen antreten.

Eine Jury vergibt für die Darbietungen bis zu 25 Punkte. Die besten Beiträge der Länderwettbewerbe werden zum Bundeswettbewerb einge-
35 laden, der jeweils im Mai oder Juni in einem anderen Bundesland ausgetragen wird.

Über 2400 Jugendliche musizieren im Bundeswettbewerb innerhalb von einer Woche in mehr als etwa 1500 Einzelwettbewerben um die besten
40 künstlerischen Leistungen in klassischer und Pop-Musik. Das Finale findet jedes Jahr in einem anderen Bundesland statt.

Aber auch für alle anderen ist die Teilnahme ein Gewinn – schon allein durch den Austausch mit
45 Musikfans von anderen Schulen und aus anderen Regionen. Betreut werden die jungen Musikerinnen und Musiker meist von ihren Lehrkräften, aber natürlich fiebern auch Eltern und Verwandte mit den Künstlern mit.

50 In jeder Runde geben die Preisträger der verschiedenen Kategorien ein Abschlusskonzert. Manchmal wird dieses sogar im Radio übertragen oder auf CD aufgezeichnet. Andere Preise können eine Einladung in das jeweilige Landesjugendensemble oder
55 zu einem Workshop, zum Beispiel „Big Band" sein.

Seit 1964 werden bei *Jugend musiziert* junge Talente entdeckt und gefördert, und einige von ihnen haben die Liebe zur Musik zum Beruf gemacht.

40

Unit 3

b) Now take notes on the following aspects to answer the questions and talk to the students about the competition "Jugend musiziert":

– who can take part in these competitions

– where they take place

– whether you have to play a certain instrument

– who selects the pieces the participants play

– how the jury evaluates the candidates

– why people should take part in such competitions

More help ➡ (p. 56/–3 Punkte)

4 Unit

It's up to you

Mein Lernplan

Datum

Was kommt dran?

Datum	Was ich lernen will	Erledigt?	Was ich noch einmal wiederholen muss/wichtige Hinweise

Unit 4

Klassenarbeit A

Gesamtpunktzahl ☐ / 70

1 LISTENING Earth Hour 🎧 / 15

a) 🔊 10 Look at the pictures. Then listen to the discussion of four students on the event of
Earth Hour and decide in which order the students mention the things depicted in the pictures. / 4

b) Listen again and decide which of the following statements is said by which student.
Tick (✓) the right box. Be careful, more than one answer can be possible. / 11

Which of the students …	Lindsay Colin	Jared McCauley	Geraldine Wasey	Cameron Howard
1 … thinks that Earth Hour is an amazing project?				
2 … doubts that Earth Hour really saves a lot of energy?				
3 … argues that taking part in Earth Hour is much more than doing nothing?				
4 … believes that Earth Hour is a great event for people all over the world to stand together for the environment?				
5 … changes their mind on the importance of Earth Hour?				
6 … supports the idea of organizing an energy-saving project at school?				

43

4 Unit

2 WORDS Saving a giant /12

Read the text and complete it with suitable phrases from the box.
Be careful with the verb forms. There are more phrases than you need.

> campaign against • demonstrate against/for • sit-in • memorable •
> discriminate against • protest (against) • take a stand on • environmental •
> take part in • rise up against • bring about • get/be involved in • intention •
> effective • take notice of • draw attention to • broadcast • suffer from

In 1997, Julia Hill joined a group of _____ activists who _____

the destruction of a large area of ancient forest by a big company. At the beginning, she climbed

a tree for a few days, but this neither impressed the company nor _____ of the media

to this initiative. But they wanted to continue to _____ saving the old trees

and the forest. The question was how? The _____ of the activists was clear:

the public should _____ their _____ cutting down this giant

redwood, so it had to be a _____ action.

Julia Hill finally broke the record of a tree _____, which at that time was for 42 days.

After about three months, her name started to be _____ on the radio and on TV.

She gave interviews and explained the importance of saving trees to the people. The action had been very

_____, but she still decided to stay in the tree.

After having lived in the tree for little more than two years, her action was successful and _____

change. The tree was saved and the company paid money which supported a school.

Unit 4

3 LANGUAGE Organizing protest
/ 12

Match the sentence halves. Decide which verb should be simple past, which past perfect progressive.

1 A group of students _____ (want) to bring about change after

a it _____ (start) to rain.

2 They _____ (discuss) different events when

b he finally _____ (find) a suitable picture for a poster.

3 A student _____ (search) for information on the internet all evening when

c they _____ (talk) about organizing an initiative for several months.

4 The speaker _____ (need) a break because

d he _____ (march) in the rain without a jacket.

5 They _____ (walk) the streets for half an hour when

e he _____ (talk) all morning.

6 The next day one of the protesters _____ (have) a really bad cold because

f one of them _____ (suggest) a march against animal testing.

4 LANGUAGE Children's rights
/ 5

You are writing for the school's newspaper and have therefore interviewed a member of
the school committee that organizes an event on children's rights.
In the next meeting of the newspaper club, you report the questions you asked. Use indirect speech.

1 Why do you want to organize an event on children's rights?

   I asked _____

2 Are you planning to invite an expert on the topic?

   I wanted to know _____

3 What will you prepare to show the violation of children's rights in the world?

   I asked _____

4 Are you going to talk about initiatives students can take?

   _____

5 What will you say about organizations for children?

   _____

4 Unit

5 LANGUAGE Taking action   / 11

Students at an English school want to take action and talk about it with their social studies teacher.
Read the text. Choose one verb from each box and complete the sentences.
Be careful with the tense of the first verb and use the gerund form for the second verb.

> (to) fancy · (to) suggest · (to) imagine · (to) mind ·
> (to) keep · (to) admit · (to) enjoy · (to) consider ·
> (to) dislike · (to) risk · (to) discuss

> (to) start · (to) join · (to) protest · (to) raise ·
> (to) get (2x) · (to) think · (to) go · (to) take (2x) ·
> (to) cycle

Our social studies class teacher asked us one day whether we could _____ a stand for

an issue we were concerned about. Some of us openly _____ for or against an issue

was something they would never do. Most of us _____ involved to be a very important

right every citizen has. They thought if people _____ their voice, they can influence

what politicians do. We agreed on the point that none of us would _____ into trouble.

One boy _____ about others so much and _____ an initiative

for the environment at school. Another one added that he would _____ action to make

our school greener. So we _____ to school every day as a first step. Even though a

few of us don't _____ by bike, they don't _____ our initiative

on two days a week for a start.

More help ➡ *(p. 57/−3 Punkte)*

6 WRITING Protecting the environment ✎   / 15

The students' magazine SPEAK UP, written by students and about students, asks young
people how they would improve the environment in their hometown if they were the town's mayor.
A jury will then decide which of the articles students can read in the next issue.

SPEAK UP – *A Magazine by Students, for Students and about Students*

We are looking for your ideas!

How would you improve the environment
in your hometown if you were the next mayor?

Grab a pen and start writing! A jury will then
decide which of your articles will be published
in our next issue.

Write an article of 150 to 200 words for the magazine's competition.

Unit 4

Klassenarbeit B

Gesamtpunktzahl ☐ / 103

1 READING Taking a stand ▯

/ 11

When talking about the topic *It's up to you!* you investigate in your class what young people can do to take a stand. You find this article in a magazine for students.

Read the text.

SPEAK UP – *A Magazine by Students, for Students and about Students*

Judith Speaks:
Why we must learn to take a stand –
one student's message to the adults of this world

The younger generation has the right to speak their minds. Whether in private or in public, their opinions are as valid and important as any adult's. Here is what one brave student has to say about why it is so
5 *important for her generation to be given opportunities to take a stand.*

A Young people of my generation are reminded every day that we are the future. Our parents tell us what our duties are regularly, and our teachers
10 speak to us about our responsibilities constantly. Nobody lets us forget that we must work hard, we must always do our best, we must be strong, we should have big dreams and we should follow those dreams. Yet how can we possibly be the future if
15 our opinions are not valued? How can we chase our dreams if we are not heard when we express our feelings honestly? And how can we contribute to society if our right to voice anger, fears and hopes are treated as childish?

20 **B** The truth is, the young people today want to be the future. We want to be responsible and we want to make a difference. So please let us have a point of view. Help us to think critically and allow us to disagree with you. Reward us for the things
25 we are good at but do not punish us for the things that we cannot do well. Discuss important subjects with us so that we learn to make good life decisions. Listen to us so that we understand there is no self-interest but a common global interest. Show us respect
30 so that we will learn to respect each other and the world we share. We care about this planet, we are smart and we are eager to succeed. We have the right to be heard.

C Let me take a stand on the issue of 'freedom'.
35 My friends and I feel very strongly about prejudice and injustice. We are interested in fighting together for global issues such as environmental pollution, animal rights, religious freedom and racial prejudice. There is no reason why we should not actively
40 take part in public demonstrations that fight for just causes or sign petitions demanding justice. For example, the young people of New Zealand could join their parents and grandparents to speak out against discrimination that prevents native Maoris
45 from living on the land of their forefathers.

D Of course we would not want to attend public protests that could be dangerous or even violent. Nevertheless, there is no reason why we should not be allowed to take a strong stand safely. Every year
50 in America, thousands of people are sent to prison for crimes they did not do. Many of these prisoners were released because people, including students, wrote letters and signed petitions to free them. This is the loudest way to fight injustice silently. We too
55 would have liked to be among the 30,000 people who signed petitions that finally allowed women to vote in 1893. Today, we could learn from 8-year-old Vivienne Harr who was shocked by photos she had seen of little boys carrying heavy rocks on their backs
60 just to earn a few cents a day. Vivienne decided to sell lemonade to raise money for them. She was so successful that in 365 days, she raised over $100,000 for her cause. We may be young but we are strong and we can make a difference. Young
65 people of the world, let's take a stand!

47

4 Unit

a) The text can be divided in paragraphs A to D. Find captions for each paragraph. / 4

A _____

B _____

C _____

D _____ **More help** ➜ *(p. 58/–2)*

b) Now look at the following statements and decide which of them are **true** and which are **false**. / 7

		true	false
1	Adults remind children of their duties regularly.	○	○
2	Even though children speak the truth, they are not allowed to have their own opinion.	○	○
3	The relationship between children and parents should be based on tolerance and respect.	○	○
4	Protest is only successful when young and old always take a stand together.	○	○
5	The author encourages young people to take part in peaceful protest.	○	○
6	Signatures by students freed all the people in America who were in prison but innocent.	○	○
7	A girl supported boys who were employed in child labour by selling lemonade.	○	○

2 WORDS Being an activist / 12

Read the text and complete it with suitable phrases from the box.
Be careful with the verb forms. There are more phrases than you need.

> (to) struggle · involved in · (to) be based on · dawn · concerned about ·
> democracy · demand for · (to) persuade · (to) gather · case · either … or ·
> attempt · safety · (to) take a break · accident · citizen

Have you ever thought of supporting your community by being a firefighter? The whole concept in small

villages and towns _____ people like you and me who are interested in and

_____ the _____ of everyone who _____

lives _____ works there, or is perhaps visiting. The _____

firefighters and their service is quite high. They are called in _____ of fire, when a street

is flooded or if there is an _____. No matter whether it's _____,

noon or midnight – they _____ to help every _____ as fast as

possible. Unfortunately, they are sometimes annoyed that some people just _____

and watch instead of helping once they get to the spot. Are you interested in getting _____

this challenging work? Just ask us!

48

Unit 4

3 WORDS It's up to you to bring about change! / 12

Look at the following sentences and complete them with the right preposition or adverb.

1 Please pay attention _____ what I am saying.

2 Her involvement _____ saving a tree made Julia Hill famous.

3 How much more proof _____ discrimination against immigrants does the

government need to take action?

4 I can't resist buying books even though my bookshelves are already taking _____

a lot of space in my house.

5 Finding a solution _____ our problem seems to be really hard.

6 Most young people buy _____ the idea that they can change the world for the better.

7 Please pass these copies _____ and take one each.

8 He probably meant to be friendly, but he didn't come _____ as a very nice person.

9 The teacher asked the students to focus _____ the answers to the questions

while listening to the dialogue.

10 When giving her presentation, Laura projected some pictures _____ the classroom wall.

11 I'm sorry, but it is really difficult for me to understand you. Could you slow _____

a bit, please?

12 I usually take no notice _____ what people write about me on social networks.

4 LANGUAGE Reporting on an interview / 17

You took the following notes while interviewing a member of the school committee that organizes
an event on children's rights. During the next meeting of the newspaper club, you use the notes
to report on the interview to the other members.

- organize an event on children's rights to make people aware of the situation of children all over the world (1 P)
- students and children in particular don't know about their rights (1 P)
- invited an expert because people pay more attention to what they say (3 P)
- already prepared large pictures because they are very emotional and affect people more (3 P)
- the organizers are hoping that people will do more for children after the event: donate money, adopt a project somewhere in the world so that children can go to school (for example in Africa), don't buy clothes made by children (6 P)
- will ask the expert to speak about UNICEF (1 P)
- this organization fights for the rights of children, for example every child should be able to go to school (2 P)

When I talked to one of the members of the school committee organizing the event on children's rights,

she told me _____

49

Unit 4

5 LANGUAGE An activist's talk / 10

You listen to a talk given by an environmental activist. Later on, you tell your class what she spoke about. Use a suitable verb from the box to report what she said. There are more verbs than you need.

> (to) advise · (to) deny · (to) invite · (to) offer · (to) promise ·
> (to) refuse · (to) suggest · (to) tell · (to) say · (to) insist · (to) state

1 Most of our actions are silent forms of protest like petitions or sit-ins which everybody can join in.
___

2 We will continue to draw people's attention to peaceful protest in the future.
___

3 We have never used any violence in our active protest.
___

4 Never ever has there been any kind of involvement in riots.
___

5 I will not go on strike. It's the wrong tactic.
___

6 We believe that it is illegal to discriminate against people because of their skin colour.
___

7 If you are interested in our initiatives, why don't you have a look at our website or talk to one of us to get more information. ___

8 I am sure that a lot of people ask the right questions and are an example to their community.
___

9 We really have to raise our voices if we want to protect the environment.
___

10 If you want to find out what's going on in your area, you can contact your local councillor.
___

More help ➡ *(p. 58/−3 Punkte)*

Unit 4

6 LANGUAGE Planning a flash mob   / 14

Some students at an American high school are talking about preparing a flash mob in a local mall.
Complete their dialogue. Choose the right form of the verbs in brackets ( ): gerund or to-infinitive.

Chloe: Well guys, remember we decided _____ (stage/perform)

the song "Going green and social" at the mall some day. What about this weekend?

Joseph: That's right. I still fancy _____ (sing)

along with you, but are you sure people will join in?

Charlotte: Yes, they will. If some of us start _____ (sing) one by one and

the other students keep _____ (fall) in, I'm sure people will like it.

Matthew: I agree, and I believe most of them know the tune. That's why people won't be thinking about

_____ (join) us for long –

they'll just begin _____ (sing)!

Charlotte: Didn't you offer _____ (bring)

your little drum to encourage people, Matthew?

Matthew: Yes, I can do that. That will help create a really good atmosphere. People won't regret

_____ (be) there.

Chloe, what else do we need _____ (bring)?

Chloe: Nothing else really. Just be there and don't forget _____ (study)

the lyrics of the song again.

Joseph: I hope we will all manage _____ (be) there on time.

Matthew: I promise _____ (stay)

close to the bakery for around 12 o'clock.

Charlotte: Oh dear! I have to admit _____ (be) on time for things

is really hard for me! I'll try _____ (give) my best!

Chloe: See you all on Saturday at 12 o'clock then!

51

4 Unit

7 MEDIATION Get involved!   / 12

Your Korean host sister has found a brochure with information on different possibilities young people in Germany have to raise their voice on political issues. She knows some German, but doesn't understand everything. So she asks you to explain the most important aspects of the two programmes to her in English.

Artikel 1
Junge Botschafter für den Frieden der Welt

Jugendliche tagen als Sicherheitsrat der Vereinten Nationen und laden zur UN-Generalversammlung ein. Sie debattieren wie große Politiker aktuelle Themen von weltpolitischer Bedeutung. Sie einigen sich auf Lösungen und verabschieden Resolutionen. All dies sind wesentliche Bestandteile des Planspiels Model United Nations (MUN) für Schülerinnen oder Studierende. Ob Deutschland, die USA, China oder ein anderes Land dieser Welt, die Teilnehmer erarbeiten sich die Position dieses Landes und vertreten es dann in den Gesprächen und Sitzungen der oft mehrtägigen Veranstaltungen. Diese finden überall in Deutschland an Schulen oder Universitäten statt. Gruppen aus aller Welt treffen sich dann und debattieren meist auf Englisch oder Deutsch. Doch es gibt auch weltweit internationale MUN-Konferenzen. Welches Ziel verfolgen diese Veranstaltungen? Zum einen üben die Teilnehmer ihre sprachlichen Fähigkeiten, sie lernen, ihre Redebeiträge wirkungsvoll zu gestalten, und probieren die Umsetzung in den Tagungen aus. Zum anderen machen sie sich mit den Zielen und Regelungen der tatsächlichen Vereinten Nationen vertraut. Sie lernen die Arbeit dieses Gremiums besser kennen und entwickeln Verständnis für andere Kulturen und deren Sichtweisen auf das weltpolitische Geschehen. Dabei stärken sie hoffentlich ihr eigenes Interesse an Politik, um weiterhin ihre Stimme zu erheben und sich später selbst zu engagieren.

Artikel 2

Zwei Jugendliche zwischen 18 und 25 Jahren vertreten Deutschlands Jugend jährlich im Oktober und Februar bei den Vereinten Nationen in New York. Ein Jahr lang sind die Vertreter in dieser Sache viel unterwegs. Ihr Engagement erfordert Interesse an Politik, insbesondere an der Arbeit der Vereinten Nationen, Enthusiasmus und ein gutes Zeitmanagement. Denn viele Termine sind unter einen Hut zu bringen: Zweimal im Jahr treffen die Delegierten auf ihrer Tour durch Deutschland Jugendliche an Schulen, in Universitäten, in Vereinen oder auch im Gefängnis, um sich in Gesprächen und Diskussionen ein Bild davon zu machen, was Jugendliche bewegt. Die Themen, die sie dabei sammeln, sind sehr vielfältig und reichen von Bildung über Klimawandel bis hin zu Armut und Kriminalität.

Seit zehn Jahren schon informieren sich jeweils zwei Vertreter über aktuelle politische und soziale Themen, sprechen mit Politikern und unterstützen die deutschen Delegierten zur Versammlung der Vereinten Nationen in New York. Sie beraten diese insbesondere zu Themen Jugendlicher und bringen ihnen deren Sichtweise näher. Doch auch sie selbst haben ein Rederecht auf zwei Konferenzen in New York und bereichern mit ihrem Blickwinkel und ihrer Kreativität die Diskussionen und das Ringen um wirksame Lösungen für die Probleme Jugendlicher in der Welt.

Unit 4

8 SPEAKING Describing and interpreting images   / 15

🔊 11 Cartoons often contain an important message and catch the audience's attention. Look at the cartoon and listen to Megan. She uses the cartoon to give a presentation on the topic *It's up to you*.

NOW YOU

You and your partner want to prepare a presentation on the topic *It's up to you* and you would like to use a cartoon to illustrate it.

Look at the following cartoon. Describe and interpret it in detail, and tell your friend why you would like to use this cartoon to present the topic.

"Would you like a bag for that?"

You can look at page 87 in your student's book. The STEPs there will help you to describe and interpret the cartoon.

53

More help

Unit 1 — Klassenarbeit A

1 READING The Stolen Generations – a long way to recognition (p. 6)

Match the sentence halves below according to the information given in the text.

- give up their Aboriginal identities/ learn the English language
- they will continue their fight for recognition
- the children who were taken away from their families and (have) suffered from it all their lives
- took children from their Aboriginal parents
- when they discuss racism and prejudice/ moral standards (in films and books) and criticize the government for its policy on Aborigines
- stay in boarding school
- they do not have equal chances to become successful people

Unit 1 — Klassenarbeit B

7 WRITING Would I like to go to the School of the Air? (p. 17)

These ideas might help you to write your argumentative text.

School of the Air	
advantages	**disadvantages**
– lessons at home, in the sun, outside	– you cannot meet your friends every day
– times for studying are more flexible	– you need to show discipline to start studying
– the school comes to you, everybody has access to education (also in remote areas)	– you can only ask teachers when both of you are online
– teachers do not have many students, give you personal feedback more often, can explain for you only	– no extracurricular/after school activities
	– technology must work

Unit 2 — Klassenarbeit B

1 READING Coast to coast (p. 24)

c) Look at the quotes from the text. They might help you to add more aspects to describe Cooper's relationship with his father.

4 'a voice that sounded like it was trying to be friendly' (l. 14–15), 'Do you want a drink?' (l. 35), 'Na, I'm fine, thanks.' (l. 36), 'avoid an argument' (l. 33–34), 'forced a smile' (l. 66), 'his voice softer' (l. 68), 'sound casual' (l. 71).

5 'You're important, son, and I want us to get along.' (l. 47–48); 'You and I haven't been getting along too well recently'(l. 39–40)

6 'a convincing display of indifference' (l. 45)

3 LANGUAGE Do you think you could …? (p. 26)

Look at the people in the pictures on p. 26 and think about who wants to ask who to do what. First imagine that the people are good friends, then imagine that they are strangers. Write down the requests in different ways. These phrases might help you. The people are good friends and say:

1 Dad, _____ me where to find the main building of the university on the map?

2 Harry, _____ on the/your phone? It's too loud and _____ your mobile in the library. You can go outside.

3 Hey Katie, _____ in front of Tower Bridge?

More help

The people are strangers and say:

1 Sorry, but _____ me how to get to the station, please?

2 Excuse me, but _____ in a low voice on the phone and go outside?

_____ your phone in the library.

3 Sorry, but _____ in front of Tower Bridge? That _____.

Unit 3   Klassenarbeit A

3 WORDS In English, please   ← *(p. 34)*

Was sagst du, wenn du ausdrücken willst …

1 … dass der letzte Termin für deine Bewerbung der nächste Freitag ist?

The _____ for my _____ is next Friday.

2 … dass es dir sehr peinlich ist, dass du den Geburtstag deines besten Freundes vergessen hast?

How _____ that I forgot my best friend's birthday.

3 … dass jemand nicht schummeln soll?

No _____, please!/Don't _____, please!

4 … dass Joshua Humor hat? Joshua has _____.

5 … dass du, je eher du mit den Hausaufgaben anfängst, desto eher fertig sein wirst?

_____ you start doing your homework, _____ you'll be finished.

6 … dass wir rechtzeitig zum Abendbrot zu Hause sein könnten, wenn wir uns beeilen?

We might be home for dinner _____ if we hurry up.

7 … dass die gegenwärtige Hitze eine Folge der Erderwärmung sein könnte?

The _____ heat might be a result of _____.

8 … dass bisher niemand wirklich weiß, was die Erderwärmung auf lange Sicht stoppen könnte?

So far nobody really knows what could stop _____.

9 … dass weder deine Mutter noch dein Vater in einer großen Firma arbeiten.

_____ my mother _____ my father work for a big _____.

10 … dass dein Bruder den Test nicht bestehen wird, wenn er nicht mehr dafür tut.

My brother will _____ the test _____ he works harder.

55

More help

Unit 3 — Klassenarbeit B

6 MEDIATION Successful musicians

(p. 40)

Jugend musiziert

Wer den richtigen Ton trifft, ist nicht nur ein wortgewandter Redner in allen Situationen, sondern kann sich auch gute Chancen beim bundesweiten Musikwettbewerb Jugend musiziert für Schüler und Jugendliche ausrechnen.

Jedes Jahr gibt es in allen Bundesländern Regional- und Landeswettbewerbe, bei denen Teilnehmerinnen und Teilnehmer ab der Grundschule bis zum 27. Lebensjahr ihr Können in verschiedenen Kategorien unter Beweis stellen. Sowohl im Bereich „Instrument" als auch im „Gesang" können sie allein, mit einem Partner oder sogar im Orchester oder Chor ihr Talent präsentieren und sich mit anderen messen.

> Where?
> Who?
> Play a certain instrument?

Dabei wechseln die Kategorien sowohl in den Regional- und Landeswettbewerben als auch im Bundeswettbewerb regelmäßig von Jahr zu Jahr leicht.

> Where?

Teilnehmerinnen und Teilnehmer können zum Beispiel in der Kategorie „Blechblasinstrumente" antreten, sich für die Teilnahme in der Kategorie „Klavier mit Begleitung Violine" entscheiden oder sie treten als „Vokalensemble" auf. Innerhalb dieser Kategorien werden verschiedene Altersgruppen unterschieden, sodass zum Beispiel die Neun- und Zehnjährigen oder die 16- und 17-Jährigen in einer Wertungsgruppe beurteilt werden.

> Play a certain instrument?

Die Teilnehmerinnen und Teilnehmer stellen sich ihr Programm für das Vorspiel selbst zusammen und müssen dabei mit originalen Werken aus verschiedenen Epochen antreten.

Eine Jury vergibt für die Darbietungen bis zu 25 Punkte. Die besten Beiträge der Länderwettbewerbe werden zum Bundeswettbewerb eingeladen, der jeweils im Mai oder Juni in einem anderen Bundesland ausgetragen wird.

> Evaluation – how?

Über 2400 Jugendliche musizieren im Bundeswettbewerb innerhalb von einer Woche in mehr als etwa 1500 Einzelwettbewerben um die besten künstlerischen Leistungen in klassischer und Pop-Musik. Das Finale findet jedes Jahr in einem anderen Bundesland statt.

> Who chooses?

Aber auch für alle anderen ist die Teilnahme ein Gewinn – schon allein durch den Austausch mit Musikfans von anderen Schulen und aus anderen Regionen. Betreut werden die jungen Musikerinnen und Musiker meist von ihren Lehrkräften, aber natürlich fiebern auch Eltern und Verwandte mit den Künstlern mit.

> Why?

In jeder Runde geben die Preisträger der verschiedenen Kategorien ein Abschlusskonzert. Manchmal wird dieses sogar im Radio übertragen oder auf CD aufgezeichnet. Andere Preise können eine Einladung in das jeweilige Landesjugendensemble oder zu einem Workshop, zum Beispiel „Big Band" sein.

> Where/When?

Seit 1964 werden bei Jugend musiziert junge Talente entdeckt und gefördert, und einige von ihnen haben die Liebe zur Musik zum Beruf gemacht.

More help

Unit 4 — Klassenarbeit A

5 LANGUAGE Taking action (p. 46)

Students at an English school want to take action and talk about it with their social studies teacher. Read the text. Complete the sentences using the correct form of the verbs in the box.

> (to) start · (to) join · (to) protest · (to) raise · (to) get (2x) · (to) think · (to) go · (to) take (2x) · (to) cycle

Our social studies class teacher asked us one day whether we could imagine _____

a stand for an issue we were concerned about. Some of us openly admitted _____

for or against an issue was something they would never do. Most of us considered _____

involved to be a very important right every citizen has. They thought if people keep _____

their voice, they can influence what politicians do. We agreed on the point that none of us would risk

_____ into trouble. One boy disliked _____

about others so much and suggested _____ an initiative for the environment at school.

Another one added that he would enjoy _____ action to make our school greener.

So we discussed _____ to school every day as a first step. Even though a few of us

don't fancy _____ by bike, they don't mind _____

our initiative on two days a week for a start.

57

More help

Unit 4 — Klassenarbeit B

1 READING Taking a stand 📄
(p. 47)

a) Look at the captions for the paragraphs of the text and decide which of them matches which paragraph best. Be careful: there are more captions than you need.

1 Fighting for global issues ○
2 Demanding rights ○
3 Successful protest ○

4 Our voice for the future ○
5 Free people whatever it takes ○
6 Help us to make a difference ○

5 LANGUAGE An activist's talk
(p. 50)

You listen to a talk given by an environmental activist. Later on, you tell your class what she spoke about. Complete the sentences below with what the environmentalist said.

1 Most of our actions are silent forms of protest like petitions or sit-ins which everybody can join in.

She said _____

2 We will continue to draw people's attention to peaceful protest in the future.

She promised _____

3 We have never used any violence in our active protest.

She insisted _____

4 Never ever has there been any kind of involvement in riots.

She denied/said _____

5 I will not go on strike. It's the wrong tactic.

She refused _____

6 We believe that it is illegal to discriminate against people because of their skin colour.

She said they believed _____

7 If you are interested in our initiatives, why don't you have a look at our website or talk to one of us to get

more information. She suggested _____

8 I am sure that a lot of people ask the right questions and are an example to their community.

She said she was sure _____

9 We really have to raise our voices if we want to protect the environment.

She insisted _____

10 If you want to find out what's going on in your area, you can contact your local councillor.

She advised _____

Generelle Lerntipps

How to do well in a test

Der nächste Test ist angekündigt? Kein Problem – solange du weißt, worauf du dich vorbereiten musst. Schaue dir dafür noch einmal die Unit in deinem Schülerbuch an und erstelle dir eine Lernlandkarte. Wenn du Hilfe benötigst, frage einen Mitschüler oder deine Englischlehrerin oder deinen Englischlehrer.
Auf der Lernlandkarte vermerkst du, was du schon kannst und was du noch üben willst.
Dann kann die Vorbereitung losgehen.

Wenn du einige Grundregeln beachtest, ist das schon der erste Schritt zum Erfolg:
- Passe im Unterricht auf, arbeite mit und stelle Fragen, wenn etwas unklar ist.
- Erledige Hausaufgaben regelmäßig und sorgfältig.
- Übe täglich 10 bis 15 Minuten – Vokabeln, Grammatik, oder was dir sinnvoll erscheint.

Zwei Wochen vor dem Test solltest du mithilfe der Lernlandkarte (oder einer anderen Übersicht) den Stoff in kleinere und übersichtliche Lernhäppchen unterteilen und dir einen Lernplan erstellen. Dazu findest du in deinem Klassenarbeitstrainer vor jeder Unit eine Tabelle, die du ausfüllen kannst.

Lies noch einmal die Texte der zuletzt durchgenommenen Unit (Part A, B, C und Text File). Fasse mündlich oder schriftlich zusammen, worum es ging.

Wiederhole den Wortschatz der Unit mithilfe des *Vocabulary*, des *Spelling Course* oder des *Wordmaster Access 5 Abschlussband*. Arbeite mit Vokabelkarteikarten, Merkzetteln, einer Mindmap oder Wortfeldern. Schreibe dir Wörter und Wortverbindungen, mit denen du immer wieder Schwierigkeiten hast, auf. Du kannst natürlich auch mit der VokabeltrainerApp und dem Vokabeltaschenbuch arbeiten.

Schaue dir noch einmal die neue Grammatik an. In der *Grammar File* findest du Regeln und Beispiele, Aufgaben zum Üben sind in den *Practice*-Abschnitten des Schülerbuches sowie im *Workbook* enthalten oder auch als interaktive Übungen zu finden.

Zwei Tage vor der Klassenarbeit solltest du mit der Vorbereitung fertig sein.
Etwas klappt doch noch nicht so richtig? Schreibe einen kurzen Text und verwende darin Wörter, die noch nicht ganz sitzen.
Lies die Texte ein weiteres Mal.
Erkläre einem Freund oder einer Freundin die neue Grammatik.

Am Abend vor dem Test entspanne dich. Gib dem Gelernten eine Chance, sich zu ordnen und zu setzen. Arbeite nicht mehr, sondern höre Musik, treibe Sport oder lies.
Gehe rechtzeitig ins Bett, damit du ausgeschlafen bist.

Am Morgen des Tests stehe in Ruhe auf und frühstücke. Lies irgendetwas Englisches zum „Aufwärmen", aber lerne oder wiederhole nichts mehr.
Du hast dich gut vorbereitet, also gibt es keinen Grund, nervös zu sein.

Während der Klassenarbeit schließlich lies dir zu Beginn alle Aufgaben durch. Löse zuerst die Aufgaben, die dir einfach erscheinen. Wende dich dann schwereren Aufgaben zu. Konzentriere dich und lasse dich nicht ablenken.
Hake Aufgaben, die du bearbeitet hast, ab. So behältst du den Überblick und siehst, wie du vorankommst.
Schaue ab und zu auf die Uhr. Du solltest für den Schluss etwas Zeit einplanen, um deine Antworten noch einmal durchzulesen und wenn nötig zu korrigieren.

Bewertungsraster

MEDIATION, SPEAKING, WRITING

MEDIATION	4	3	2	1

Content
I cover the important points in the task. The information is correct and complete.
I explain cultural differences.

Situation
I understand the situation I am in and speak/write accordingly.
I have in mind who I am speaking to/writing for. I sum up information.

Language
I use special vocabulary for the topic. I paraphrase words I don't know/
find synonyms or opposites. I join the different aspects of the topic/sentences
with linking words. My grammar is correct.

SPEAKING – Monologisches Sprechen	5	4	3	2	1

Content
I cover the important points in the task. The information is new/interesting/original/
complete. I give examples/details. I give my opinion and arguments for it.

Structure
My introduction leads the listener to the topic.
In the introduction I also say what the text is about.
My presentation follows a clear structure. My ideas follow a logical order.
I illustrate my main points on a poster/the blackboard/with pictures/things/a song/…
I sum up the main information at the end.
I can answer possible questions on my presentation.

Language and delivery
I use special vocabulary for the topic. I use different adjectives and adverbs.
I join the different aspects of my topic/sentences with linking words.
I pronounce words correctly. My grammar is correct.
I make eye contact. I use notes/a crib sheet.
I speak clearly and at a normal pace/fluently.

WRITING	5	4	3	2	1

Content
I cover the important points in the task.
The information is new/interesting/original/complete.
I give examples/details. I give my opinion and arguments for it.

Structure
My introduction leads the reader to the topic.
In the introduction I also say what the text is about.
I use paragraphs. Each paragraph has a new idea. My ideas follow a logical order.
There is a conclusion to my text. I have in mind who will read the text.

Language
I use special vocabulary for the topic. I use different adjectives and adverbs.
I join sentences with linking words. I spell words correctly. (I check them in a dictionary.)
I write simple and complex sentences and my grammar is correct.

Notentabelle

Diese Tabellen sollen dir bei der Bewertung deiner Übungsklassenarbeiten helfen.
Möglicherweise legt deine Lehrerin oder dein Lehrer einen anderen Bewertungsmaßstab zugrunde.

Gesamtpunktzahl 65

Note	1	2	3	4	5	6
Punkte	65–62	61,5–52	51,5–39	38,5–26	25,5–13,5	13–0

Gesamtpunktzahl 67

Note	1	2	3	4	5	6
Punkte	67–64	63,5–54	53,5–40,5	40–27	26,5–13,5	13–0

Gesamtpunktzahl 68

Note	1	2	3	4	5	6
Punkte	68–65	64,5–54,5	54–41	40,5–27,5	27–14	13,5–0

Gesamtpunktzahl 70

Note	1	2	3	4	5	6
Punkte	70–66,5	66–56	55,5–42	41,5–28	27,5–14	13,5–0

Gesamtpunktzahl 74

Note	1	2	3	4	5	6
Punkte	74–70,5	70–59,5	59–44,5	44–30	29,5–15	14,5–0

Gesamtpunktzahl 80

Note	1	2	3	4	5	6
Punkte	80–76	75,5–64	63,5–48	47,5–32	31,5–16	15,5–0

Gesamtpunktzahl 85

Note	1	2	3	4	5	6
Punkte	85–81	80,5–68	67,5–51	50,5–34	33,5–17	16,5–0

Gesamtpunktzahl 103

Note	1	2	3	4	5	6
Punkte	103–98	97,5–82,5	82–62	61,5–41,5	41–21	20,5–0

Tracklist

Hörverstehens-, Sprech- und Mediationaufgaben

Die Texte für die Listening- und Speaking-Aufgaben findest du auf www.scook.de.
Zum Einloggen auf Scook benötigst du den Code von Seite 1 dieses Heftes.

Track	Unit	Buchseite	Titel		Einzellaufzeit
01	Unit 1	09	SPEAKING	A visit to Australia	2:05
02–03	Unit 1	11	LISTENING	A radio show: people in the outback	6:31; 5:47
04	Unit 2	19	LISTENING	A radio programme on the science of twins	7:06
05	Unit 2	28	MEDIATION	Building bridges!	3:21
06	Unit 2	28	SPEAKING	Talking about statistics – using the internet	2:00
07	Unit 3	35	MEDIATION	My future career	3:59
08	Unit 3	35	SPEAKING	Useful information	0:52
09	Unit 3	36	LISTENING	Interview on work experience	3:35
10	Unit 4	43	LISTENING	Earth hour	6:42
11	Unit 4	53	SPEAKING	Describing and interpreting images	2:32

More than just words
Das Oxford Schulwörterbuch

Nie mehr sprachlos: Mit dem *Oxford Schulwörterbuch* immer die richtigen Worte finden – schon ausprobiert?

NEU

Das Original – Qualität aus Oxford

- Wörterbuch auf aktuellem Sprachstand mit vielen Beispielsätzen – jetzt mit **Online-Wörterbuch**

- **Mediation study pages** erweitern den Wortschatz – mit allgemeinen Tipps zur Sprachmittlung und Redemitteln für häufige Situationen

- **iWriter** verbessert die Schreibkompetenz – mit Mustertexten zum Planen, Schreiben und Überarbeiten sowie Hinweisen zu Register und Stil

ISBN 978-0-19-439687-5

Das Schulwörterbuch für die Klassen 5 bis 10 entspricht den Kompetenzstufen A2-B1 des Gemeinsamen europäischen Referenzrahmens.

Weitere Informationen unter
cornelsen.de/oxford/schulwoerterbuch

Cornelsen

Impressum

English G Access Band 5 Abschlussband, Klassenarbeitstrainer

Im Auftrag des Verlages herausgegeben von:
Prof. Jörg Rademacher, Mannheim

Erarbeitet von:
Katrin Häntzschel, Wiesa

In Zusammenarbeit mit der Englischredaktion:
Stefan Höhne (Projektleitung)
Ursula Fleischhauer (verantwortliche Redakteurin)
sowie Sophie Dupiech (Bildredaktion) und Jason Shilcock

Beratende Mitwirkung:
Prof. Jörg Rademacher, Mannheim

Illustrationen:
Michael Fleischmann, Waldegg

Umschlaggestaltung:
kleiner & bold, Berlin; hawemannundmosch, Berlin; Klein & Halm Grafikdesign, Berlin

Layout und technische Umsetzung:
Ungermeyer, grafische Angelegenheiten

Tonaufnahmen: Clarity Studio Berlin
Produzent: Christian Schmitz
Tontechnik: Hüseyin Dönertaş, Pascal Thinius
Sprecher/innen: Shaunessy Ashdown, Damían García Correa, Angelina Geisler, Mumta Mala Ghedia, Melissa Holroyd, Manon Kahle, Guda Koster, Lixue Lin, Angus McGruther, Justin Reddig, Christian Schmitz, Peter Scollin, Darren Smith, Lee Stripe, Amandine Thiriet, Louise Watts, Wolfgang Zechmayer

www.cornelsen.de
www.englishg.de/access

1. Auflage, 1. Druck 2017

© 2017 Cornelsen Verlag GmbH, Berlin

Das Werk und seine Teile sind urheberrechtlich geschützt. Jede Nutzung in anderen als den gesetzlich zugelassenen Fällen bedarf der vorherigen schriftlichen Einwilligung des Verlages.

Hinweis zu den §§ 46, 52a UrhG: Weder das Werk noch seine Teile dürfen ohne eine solche Einwilligung eingescannt und in ein Netzwerk eingestellt werden. Dies gilt auch für Intranets von Schulen und sonstigen Bildungseinrichtungen.

Soweit in diesem Lehrwerk Personen fotografisch abgebildet sind und ihnen von der Redaktion fiktive Namen, Berufe, Dialoge und Ähnliches zugeordnet oder diese Personen in bestimmte Kontexte gesetzt werden, dienen diese Zuordnungen und Darstellungen ausschließlich der Veranschaulichung und dem besseren Verständnis des Inhalts.

Druck: H. Heenemann, Berlin

ISBN 978-3-06-033745-3

PEFC zertifiziert
Dieses Produkt stammt aus nachhaltig bewirtschafteten Wäldern und kontrollierten Quellen.
www.pefc.de
PEFC/04-31-1156

Titelbild: F1online; Shutterstock/Wouter Tolenaars

Illustrationen: **Michael Fleischmann,** Waldegg (S. 3; S. 7; S. 9; S. 12; S. 16; S. 17; S. 22; S. 25; S. 26; S. 27; S. 29; S. 36; S. 38; S. 43; S. 51; S. 59; Lösungen: S. 10; S. 16; S. 18; S. 24; S. 28)

Bildquellen: S. 2, Unit 1 Fotolia/totajla; Unit 2 Fotolia/Franz Pfluegl; Unit 3 Shutterstock/Syda Productions; Unit 4 Shutterstock/Brian A Jackson; S. 4 o. Fotolia/totajla; S. 8 li. Fotolia/totajla; Mi. Fotolia/artistrobd; re. o. Fotolia/artistrobd; re. u. Fotolia/laufer; S. 9 u. li. Fotolia/ronnybas; u. Mi. Fotolia/aussieanouk; u. re. Fotolia/daigor; S. 10 o. Shutterstock/Monkey Business Images; Mi. Fotolia/Nejron Photo; u. Shutterstock/Monkey Business Images; S. 14 o. li. Shutterstock/Aleksandar Todorovic; o. re. Fotolia/AustralianCamera; u. li. Fotolia/HLPhoto; u. re. Shutterstock/ChameleonsEye; S. 18 o. Fotolia/Franz Pfluegl; S. 29 o. Fotolia/rod5150; u. Fotolia/blackzheep; S. 30 o. Shutterstock/Syda Productions; S. 33 u. Fotolia/deagreez; S. 34 li. Fotolia/nirutft; re. Shutterstock/Ai825; S. 37 o. Fotolia/Focus Pocus LTD; u. li. Fotolia/connel_design; u. re. Fotolia/ajr_images; S. 39 o. Shutterstock/David Hanlon; Mi. Fotolia/FomaA; u. Fotolia/baibaz; S. 40 u. Shutterstock/Alexandru Nika; S. 44 o. imago/UPI Photo; S. 50 u. Fotolia/lightpoet; S. 52 o. re. Shutterstock/Jeff Schultes; u. re. Fotolia/Nejron Photo; o. li. PantherMedia/Viktor Cap; u. li. Shutterstock/Coprid; S. 53 o. CartoonStock/Fran; u. CartoonStock/Royston Robertson; S. 57 u. Fotolia/Kara; **Lösungen**: S. 3 o. Fotolia/totajla; S. 4 li. Fotolia/totajla; S. 4 re. Fotolia/totajla; S. 5 li. Shutterstock/Monkey Business Images; S. 5 Mi. Fotolia/Nejron Photo; S. 5 re. Shutterstock/Monkey Business Images; S. 9 o. li. Shutterstock/Aleksandar Todorovic; o. re. Fotolia/AustralianCamera; u. li. Fotolia/HLPhoto; u. re. Shutterstock/ChameleonsEye; S. 11 o. Fotolia/Franz Pfluegl; S. 18 u. li. Fotolia/blackzheep; u. re. Fotolia/rod5150; S. 19 o. Shutterstock/Syda Productions; S. 23 o. Fotolia/Focus Pocus LTD; u. li. Fotolia/connel_design; u. re. Fotolia/ajr_images; S. 26 Shutterstock/Alexandru Nika; S. 27 o. Shutterstock/Brian A Jackson; S. 29 Mi. imago/UPI Photo; S. 32 u. Shutterstock/Jeff Schultes; S. 33 u. li. CartoonStock/Fran; u. re. CartoonStock/Royston Robertson

Textquellen: S. 20–22 David Fermer *Coast to Coast,* Cornelsen Verlag